# The English Channel

by Diana Wales

**PEARSON**

**Scott Foresman**

Editorial Offices: Glenview, Illinois • Parsippany, New Jersey • New York, New York
Sales Offices: Needham, Massachusetts • Duluth, Georgia • Glenview, Illinois
Coppell, Texas • Ontario, California • Mesa, Arizona

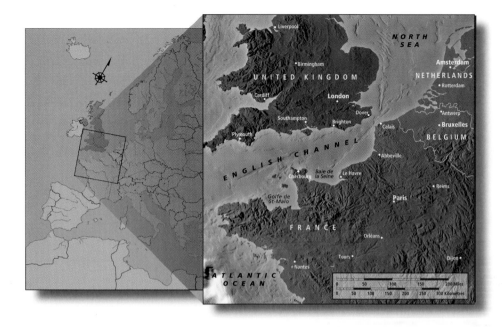

The English Channel is a narrow body
of water. It separates the southern coast of
England from the northern coast of France.

**The English Channel is busy daily with trade ships.**

The English Channel is about 350 miles long. Its widest point is 150 miles wide. Its narrowest point is 21 miles wide.

Today, the English Channel links northern Europe with the rest of the world. Many kinds of goods are carried through the Channel each day.

There are many ways to cross the English Channel. You can sail by ferry boat. You can fly in a plane. You can even travel by train in a tunnel below the English Channel.

But some more daring people choose to swim across!

**The "Chunnel" is a railroad tunnel beneath the English Channel.**

**The first man to cross the English Channel by plane was Louis Bleriot in 1909.**

**Many ferry boats cross the Channel each day.**

The English Channel is not very deep. The waves are usually not high.

You might think that these conditions make it a great place for sailing and swimming, but the waters can be extremely rough and choppy.

That's because currents from the North Sea meet currents from the Atlantic Ocean. When they join with strong winds, the water is stirred up.

The currents are strong. Wind whips across the water. There is always a chance that a swimmer could drown. Some swimmers see these wild waters as a challenge.

**Many channel swimmers covered themselves in lard to protect against the cold water.**

**Matthew Webb died in 1883. He tried to swim below Niagara Falls.**

Many people have tried to swim across the channel and drowned. In 1875, a man named Matthew Webb of the United Kingdom was the first to do so with success. Webb performed the amazing swim from England to France without stopping, in less than 22 hours.

In 1926, Gertrude Ederle of the United States became the first woman to swim across the English Channel. The Olympic medal holder swam from France to England in less than 15 hours. That was an awesome feat! She broke the men's record of that period by two hours.

**Gertrude Ederle won three medals at the 1924 Olympics.**

Since those early attempts, swimmers have continued the tradition of crossing the channel. Some make the long journey alone. Others are part of a team of two or more swimmers.

During the swim, a pilot in a boat rides alongside the swimmer. The pilot feeds the swimmer and makes sure he or she is safe.

**Relay teams join up to cross the channel together.**

Swimmers train for a long time before trying to swim the channel. They practice their swimming strokes. This helps them build endurance for long-distance swims. They also must prepare themselves for swimming in very cold water.

**Many channel swimmers are escorted by boats in case they run into trouble.**

Many people have been successful at swimming across the English Channel. Some have even done so three times without stopping. That difficult task seems like something to celebrate. If you have the stamina, the skill, and the desire for a challenge, would you consider swimming the English Channel?

**A team of Japanese mothers who swam the English Channel in 1999**